This book is dedicated to Kim and Nicole. Sorry for bothering you both so much but you have no idea how much you helped me. I love you both.

The following content is a parody, created for entertainment purposes only. It is a fictional representation and should not be taken as factual. This work is in no way affiliated with, endorsed by, or representative of the original source material or its creators. Any similarities to real-life events, people, or organizations are coincidental and not intended to be taken as literal interpretations. This parody is not meant to defame or infringe upon the rights and reputations of any persons, living or deceased, or entities involved with the original work.

Table of Contents

5...The italian princess and the very rude guest.
7...Princess Pinot and the magical turtle juice.
9...Princess woohoo and the small family carriage.
11...Princess shee and the evil party planner.
13...The countess and the two-timing prince.
15...Princess clip and the trip to blue stone manor.
17...Princess ponytail and the haunted dinner party.
19...Princess jellybean and the very scary island.
21...Princess pump and the awful employees.
23...Princess candi and the sword dual.
25...Princess diamond and the 25,000 gold coin sunglasses.
27...Princess turtle and the cursed bunny.
29...Princess baby gorgeous and the hot mic fairy.
31...Princess laviva and the big secret.

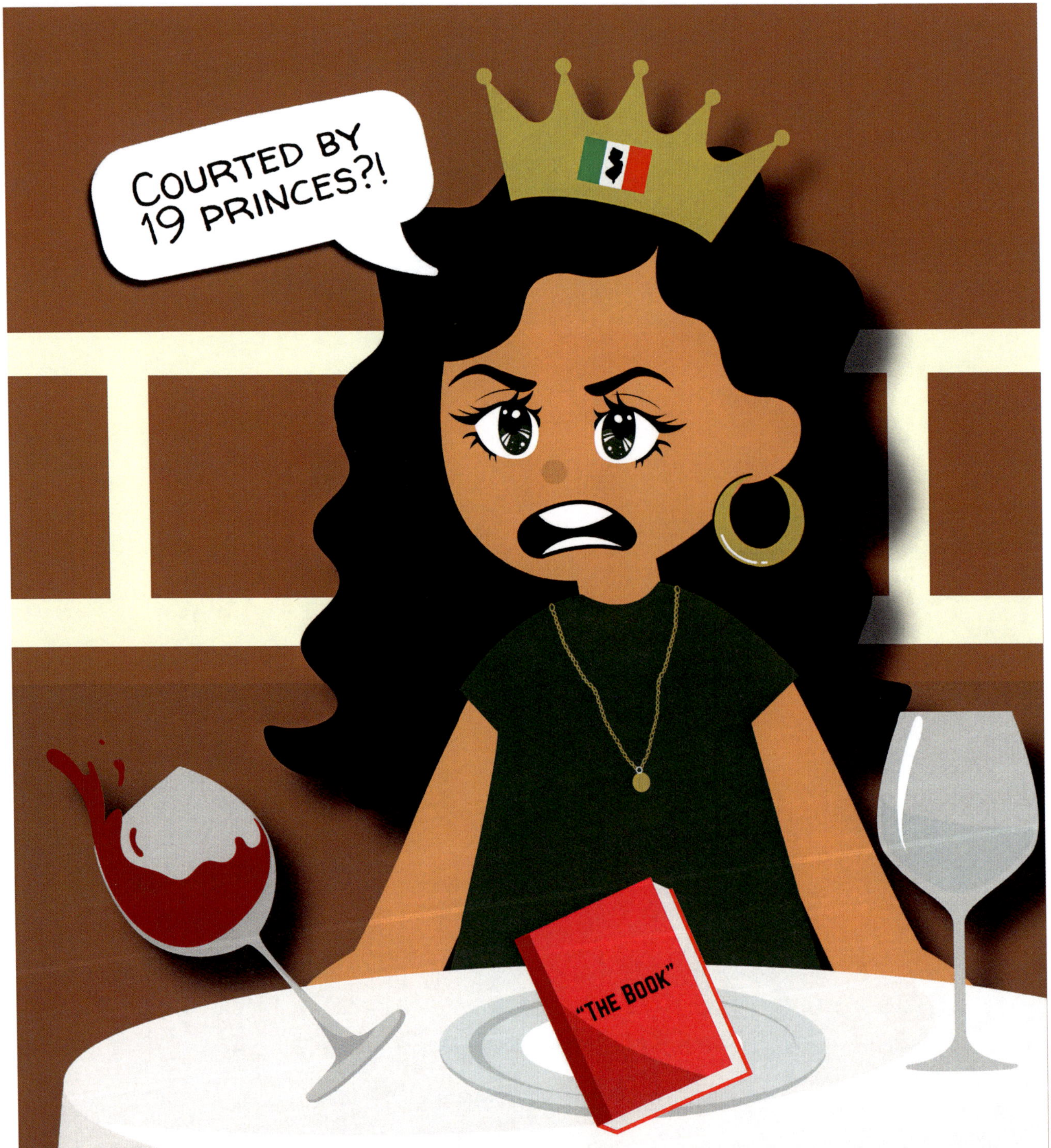
COURTED BY 19 PRINCES?!
"THE BOOK"

The Italian Princess
AND THE VERY RUDE GUEST.

Once upon a time, a princess named Tre lived in the magical kingdom of New Jersey. To celebrate building a new castle, she took all the other princesses out to dinner.

All Tre wanted was a peaceful dinner with her friends. Unfortunately, the Drama Duchess had other plans. The Duchess wanted to use the dinner party to confront the other princesses about a secret book they had found. The book revealed the Duchess used to be an evil witch and that 19 princes had courted her.

Princess Tre was shocked about the Duchess's past but even more mad that the Duchess had ruined her dinner party! She was so angry that she flipped over the entire dinner table. Princess Tre's temper ruined her dinner party.

After Princess Tre had a chance to cool down, she realized her mistake and apologized to her friends. She understood that losing her temper was not the right thing to do. She invited everyone back to her new castle for a homemade meal made with the finest "ingredientses".

Everyone except the Drama Duchess.

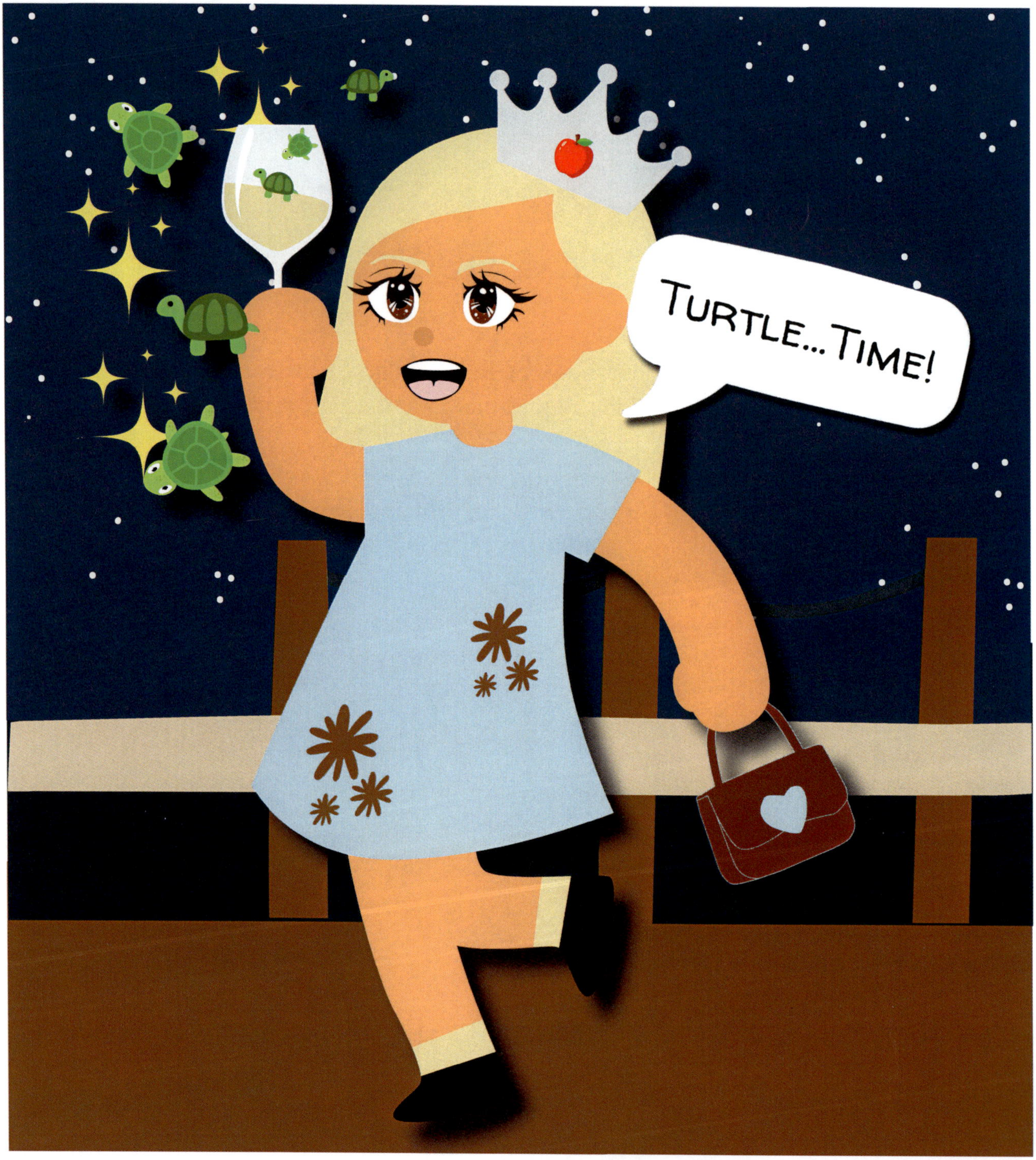
TURTLE...TIME!

Princess Pinot
AND THE MAGICAL TURTLE JUICE.

Princess Pinot and all the other New York princesses needed a vacation. The faraway kingdom of St. Johns was just the place for the overworked princess. The New York princesses spent their day soaking up the sun and swimming in the beautiful water.

When night fell, they started getting ready for dinner when a mysterious boat pulled up. Princess Pinot and her best friend, Princess Lifestyle Brand, were immediately suspicious. However, their curiosity got the better of them, and they went to inspect the ship.

An older prince and several gorgeous princesses greeted Pinot and LB. "Hello! We want to offer you our magical turtle juice!" said the prince. "What is magical turtle juice?" asked Princess Pinot. "It will help you relax," said the prince. Relax was the only word Pinot needed to hear, so she immediately started sipping her juice.

Before she knew it, magical dancing turtles started swirling around her, telling her it was time to dance. "It's turtle time!!" said one of the dancing turtles. Pinot had never felt more relaxed in her life. She started dancing and singing with the turtles. "It's turtle time. It's turtle time!" Princess Pinot got all the other princesses to join, and before they knew they were having a dance party.

The following day, the princesses woke up sick. Their heads hurt, and they were weak. "Our jewels are gone!" Princess Lifestyle Brand yelled. "Oh no! The prince must have stolen our jewels!" said Princess Pinot. That is when she realized the prince was a pirate and the magical turtle juice was a trick to distract them. "At least we have each other," Princess Lifestyle Brand said. LB was right; jewels didn't matter. Only their friendship did. The princesses agreed never to drink magical turtle juice from a stranger again.

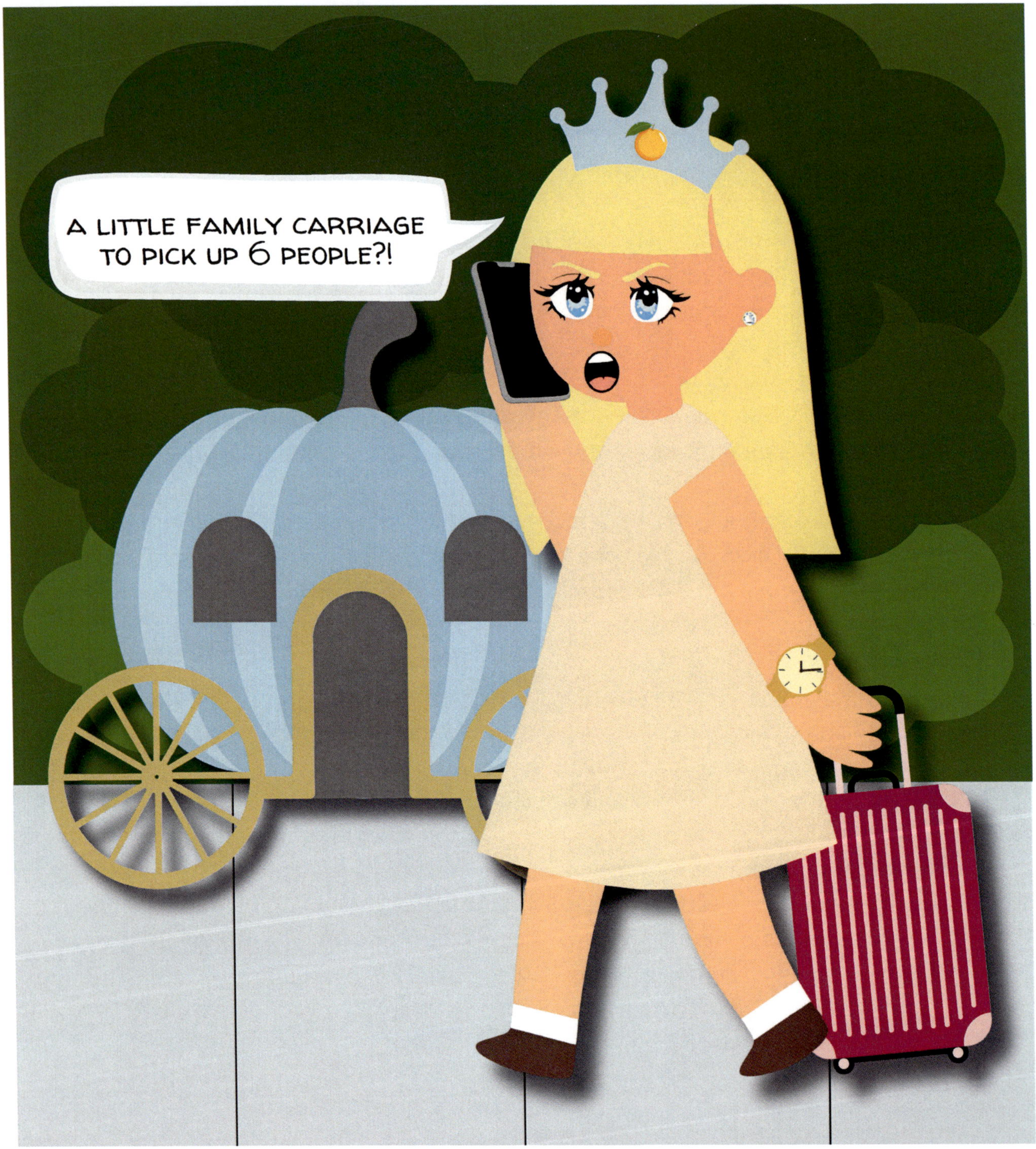
A LITTLE FAMILY CARRIAGE TO PICK UP 6 PEOPLE?!

Princess Woohoo
AND THE LITTLE FAMILY CARRIAGE.

The gated kingdom of Orange County is home to one of the first princesses of Housewifeland, Princess Woohoo. Not only was Woohoo a Princess of Orange County, but she was also the queen of her very own horse insurance empire.

Princess Woohoo was preparing for her annual family vacation, a two-week cruise around other kingdoms. She didn't want to leave any luxuries at home, so she packed all her finest gowns and jewelry. No suitcase was too large for the queen of horse insurance, and Woohoo had already arranged for the finest horse carriage to take them to their destination.

When Princess Woohoo and her five other guests stepped outside to greet their carriage, Woohoo was shocked by its size—it was so tiny! "This can't be! I am the queen of horse insurance and should have the grandest carriage in all the land! How are we supposed to all fit in this small carriage?" She yelled as she called customer service. She demanded they send a new carriage immediately.

"If we wait for a new carriage, we will miss our trip!" cried one of her guests. "If we all give up some of our dresses and jewels, we can make everything fit," another guest suggested. "We can even share some of our gowns!"

Princess Woohoo, who had been so focused on herself, stopped and looked at her family, realizing that her trip with them was much more important than taking all her gowns and jewels. She unpacked some of her stuff and hopped into the small family carriage, ready for her vacation.

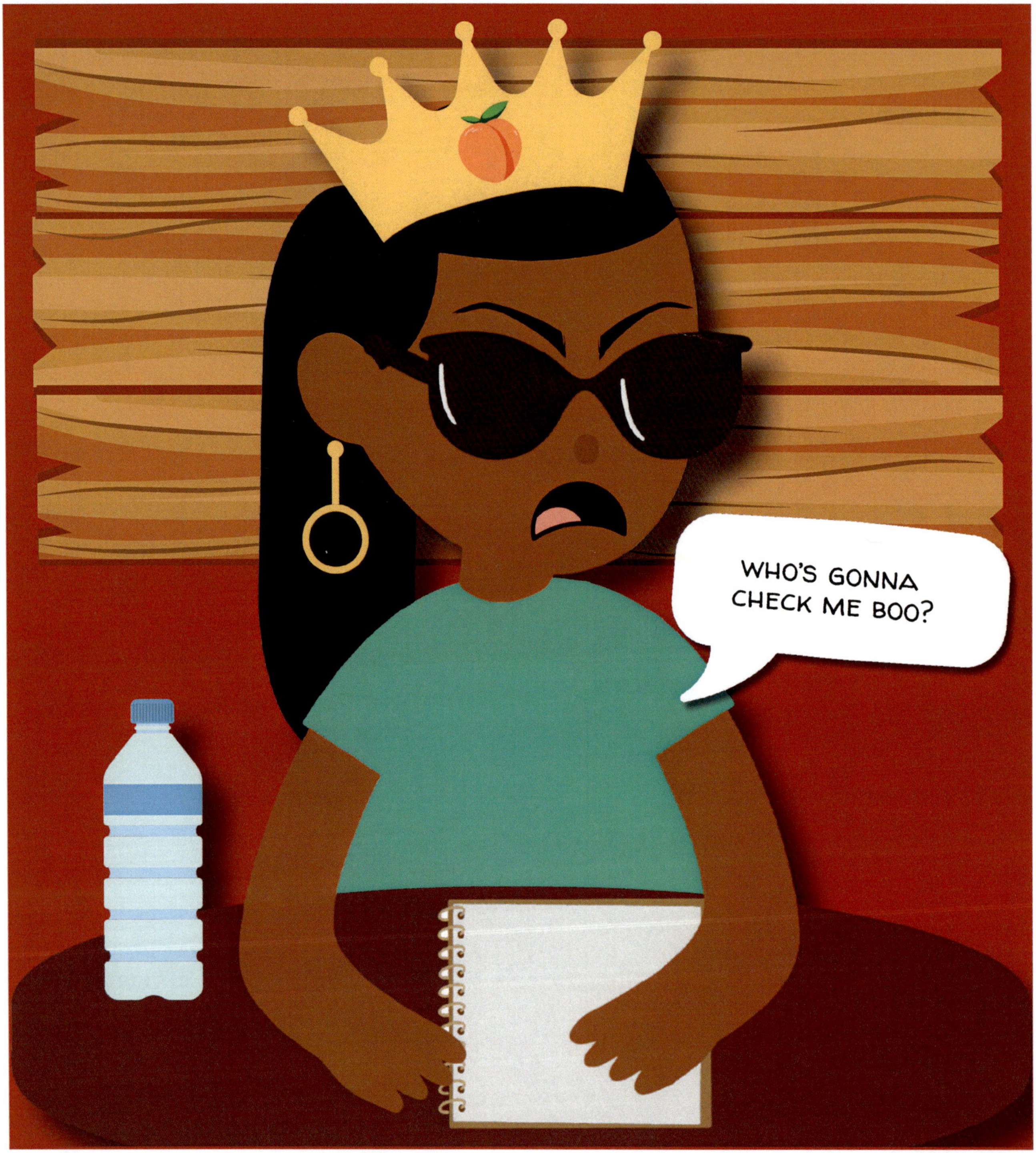
WHO'S GONNA CHECK ME BOO?

Princess Shee
AND THE EVIL PARTY PLANNER.

Once upon a time, a beautiful princess named Shee lived in Atlanta. A prince had recently broken Princess She's heart, and she wanted to put that all behind her and forget about princes. Shee thought what would be a better way to celebrate her freedom from silly princes than with an independence party!

Princess Shee, being a princess, wasn't used to doing things on her own. The princess knew she would need a party planner immediately and decided to hire the best one in the kingdom, Sir Tony. At first, Sir Tony seemed like the perfect party planner, but Princess Shee slowly realized he disliked all her ideas.

As the days passed, Princess Shee felt like her independence party was becoming Sir Tony's, not hers. The princess knew she had to take a stand. She had to fire Sir Tony and plan her own party for the first time in her life.

Princess Shee marched over to Sir Tony's castle and told him he was too bossy. The princess was going to do this on her own. It was an independence party, after all. Sir Tony became very insulted and told Princess Shee to watch herself before she got checked. The princess stood up and yelled, "Who's gonna check me, boo?" and stormed off.

Shee was so proud of herself for standing up to the mean party planner that the princess was ready to take charge and plan her party. Shee pulled in other princesses around Atlanta to help, and in the end, everything came out perfect—exactly as the princess wanted.

"PLEASE DON'T LET IT BE ABOUT PRINCE TIM."

The Countess
AND THE TWO-TIMING PRINCE.

Everything in the Countess's life had been going perfectly lately. Being a single princess in the kingdom of New York wasn't easy, but the Countess had found her Prince Charming. She was finally engaged to Prince Tim, who was everything the princess had been dreaming of.

There was only one problem: she felt the other princesses weren't happy for her. Trying to ignore a gut feeling that something was wrong, The Countess went along with the other New York princesses and took a beautiful vacation in the kingdom of Miami.

On the last day of the trip, all the princesses sat down and told the Countess they needed to talk to her. "Please don't let it be about Prince Tim," the Countess cried to her friends. The other princesses looked back at her sadly and said, "It's about Prince Tim."

"We have all kissed Prince Tim before," the princesses told The Countess. At first, he seems like a lovely prince, but once you kiss him, he turns into a toad!" The Countess couldn't believe it. "You are all jealous!" she shouted and ran out of the room.

"I have a picture to prove it!" said Princess Beth as she chased after the Countess. The Countess couldn't believe her eyes; her handsome prince was nothing but a toad. "I'm sorry I accused you girls of being jealous," the Countess told the other princesses.

That is when The Countess realized she didn't need a prince to make her life perfect. All she needed was good friends like the other princesses of New York.

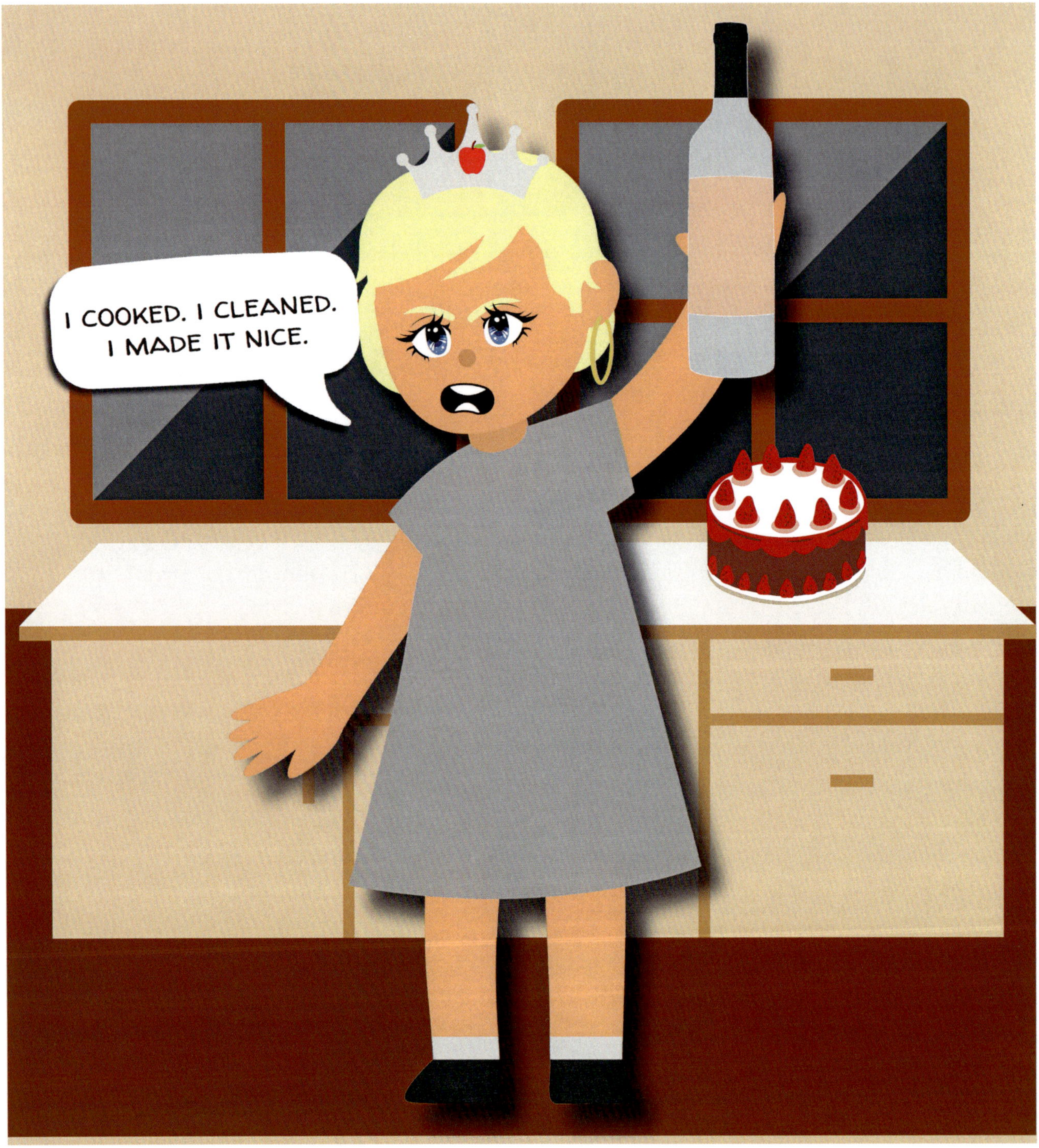
I COOKED. I CLEANED.
I MADE IT NICE.

Princess Clip
AND THE TRIP TO BLUE STONE MANOR.

Once upon a time, a princess named Clip lived in the kingdom of New York. Princess Clip always tried to be a good friend to other New York princesses. Her favorite thing to do was host a great dinner party with all her friends. With the holidays coming up, Princess Clip wanted to treat the girls to a nice trip to one of her many castles.

She invited all the princesses to her favorite holiday house, the Blue Stone Manor, in the Berkshires kingdom. Clip prepared for their arrival by cooking, cleaning, and baking a cake. When the girls arrived, Clip noticed that Princess Beth and the Countess were unhappy.

Princess Beth and the Countess wouldn't sit at the table when it was time for dinner. Instead, they began to argue. "You copied my haircut!" the Countess exclaimed. "I did not! My hair doesn't even look like yours!" Beth yelled back. The other princesses were now uncomfortable and didn't want to eat the dinner Princess Clip cooked either.

"Stop this right now!" Princess Clip got up and yelled. "I cooked, I cleaned, I made it nice! If you can't behave yourselves, then you can all go home!" Clip looked at the Countess. "Who cares if Princess Beth copied your haircut? That only means she likes the way it looks. You should take it as a compliment."

"Wow, you are right, Princess Clip. I am sorry, Princess Beth. I am also sorry to you, Clip, for ruining your dinner party," the Countess said. "I am sorry too," said Princess Beth, realizing that arguing during someone's dinner wasn't right. The princesses laughed it off, realizing that Clip was right. They finally began eating the delicious dinner that Princess Clip had prepared. They enjoyed the rest of the trip, free from any drama.

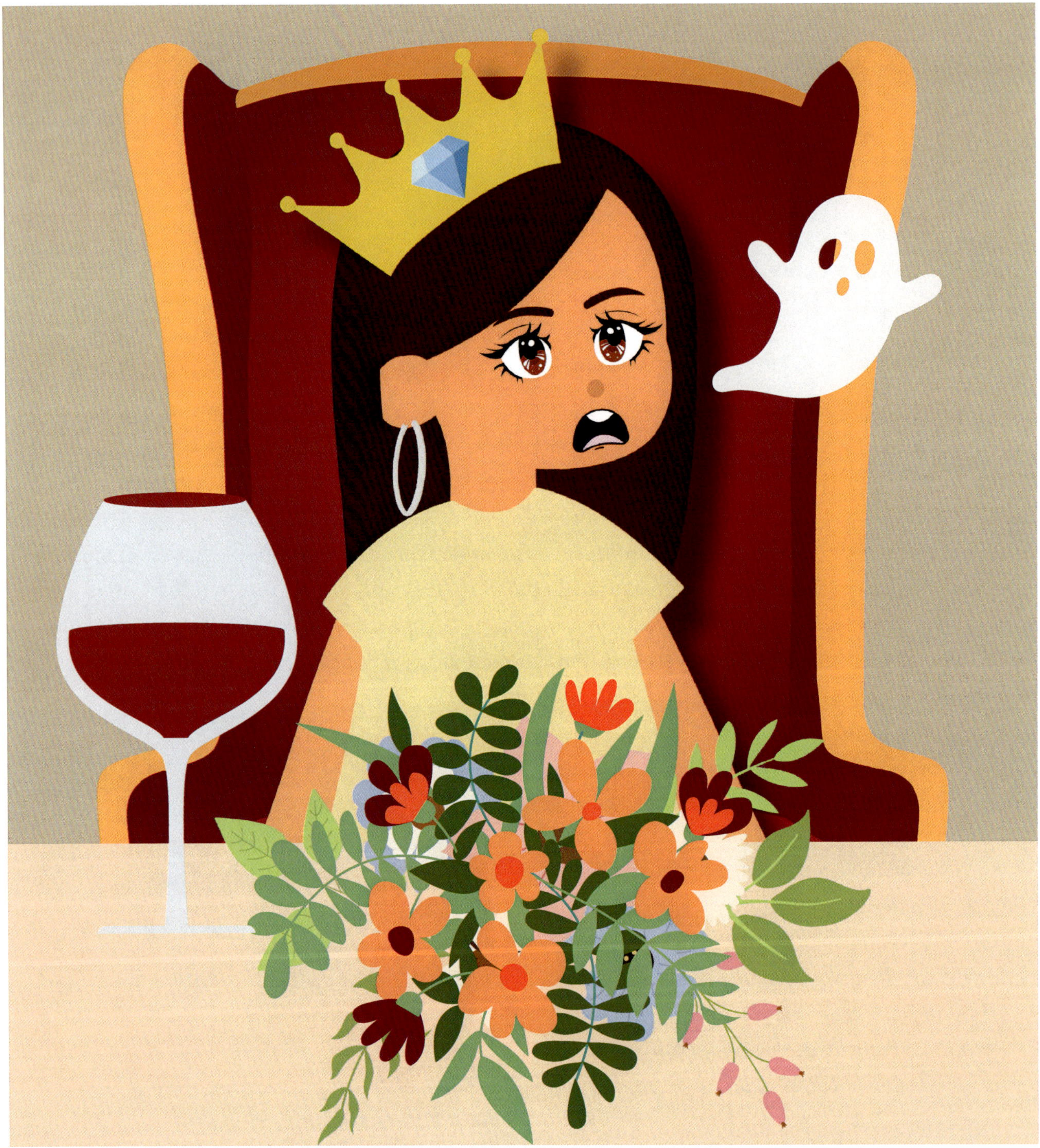

Princess Ponytail
AND THE HAUNTED DINNER PARTY.

The kingdom of Beverly Hills was very exclusive, and Princess Ponytail was one of the most popular princesses in town. One day, Princess Ponytail was invited to a dinner party at Princess Cami's castle. Ponytail thought it was an excellent opportunity to introduce some of her old friends to some of her new friends.

Princess Ponytail brought one of her oldest friends, Princess Ray, with her. When they arrived at the party, they noticed one of Princess Cami's friends giving them the cold shoulder. Princess Ponytail thought maybe all she had to do was introduce herself, so she walked right up to the princess. "This is Princess Vaporina," said Cami. "She has special powers and can talk to ghosts."

Princess Vaporina quickly walked away when the lights began to flicker. "Oh no, it's happening!" Vaporina shrieked. "The ghosts are talking to me again and telling me Princess Ponytail and Princess Ray are evil. They told me to warn you all to stay away from them!" Princess Ponytail was shocked. She wasn't evil; how could this ghost say that about her? "Can you ask the ghost what we did wrong?" Ponytail asked.

Vaporina started to walk away when the lights began to flicker again. Princess Ray tapped Ponytail on the shoulder and whispered, "Look! Princess Vaporina is flickering the lights herself." "Princess Vaporina, there isn't a ghost, is there?" Said Princess Ponytail. "We caught you flickering the lights yourself." Princess Vaporina looked embarrassed. "It is true. There is no ghost. I don't have many friends, and sometimes I do that for attention. I saw how close you and Princess Ray were and how many friends you have. I was very jealous because I do not."

"Princess Vaporina, that is so silly. We would love to be your friend!" said Ponytail. Next time you feel lonely, just be yourself. You will make more friends that way. Princess Vaporina never had trouble making any friends again.

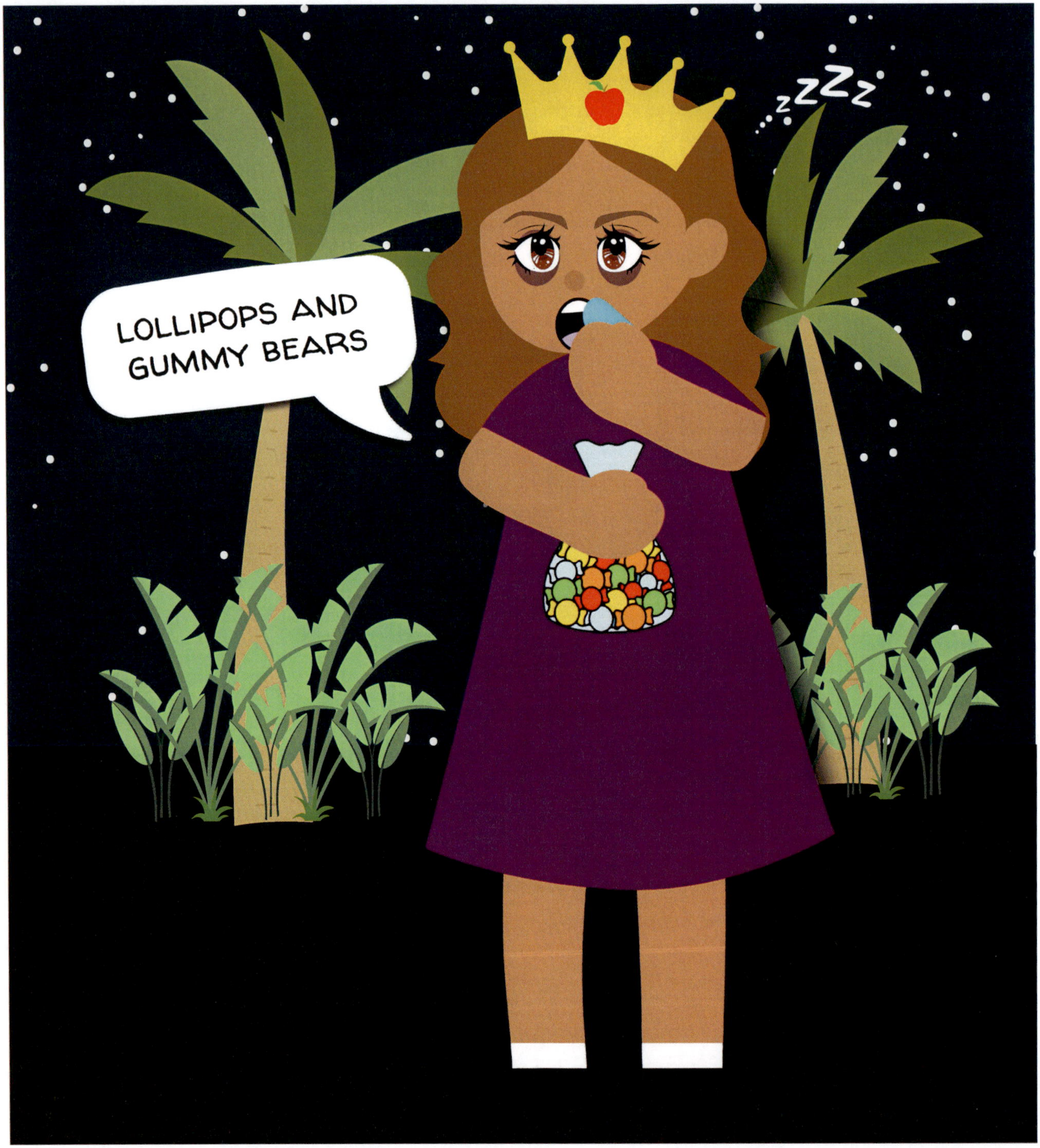
LOLLIPOPS AND GUMMY BEARS
zZZZ

Princess Jellybean
AND THE VERY SCARY ISLAND.

Princess Jellybean of New York was always afraid of sleeping away from home. She felt safe in her castle and didn't like leaving the kingdom of New York. This became a problem when the other princesses went on trips. The girls were planning a trip to the kingdom of St. Johns, and Jellybean would face her fears so she didn't miss out this time.

When the day of the trip arrived, Princess Jellybean couldn't eat anything besides candy. Jellybean ate candy when she was nervous, and she thought it would help her calm down during the trip, so she packed all her bags of jellybeans, lollipops, and gummy bears.

Princess Jellybean tried to have fun but missed New York. She continued to eat candy to help her feel better, but by the third day, she started to feel weird. "All the princesses hate me." thought Jellybean. All of a sudden, she saw the princess's faces changing. "Am I stuck on a haunted island?" Jellybean panicked.

"I need to get out of here!" Princess Jellybean yelled, and she ran past the other princesses. "What is going on?" the other princesses asked with concern. "You aren't really my friends. You are shapeshifting creatures!" Princess Jellybean declared. "What are you talking about?" Princess Beth asked, her voice filled with concern. It was then that Beth noticed all the candy Jellybean had been eating.

"Have you slept and eaten anything besides candy?" Princess Beth asked Jellybean. Princess Jellybean stopped to think. No, she had only been eating candy, which had kept her up all night. "You need to go to sleep, Princess Jellybean," said Beth. "Oh no, you are right. Tonight, I am going to eat a healthy dinner and get a good night's rest," Jellybean cried. The following day, Princess Jellybean felt great and enjoyed the rest of her vacation without the help of candy.

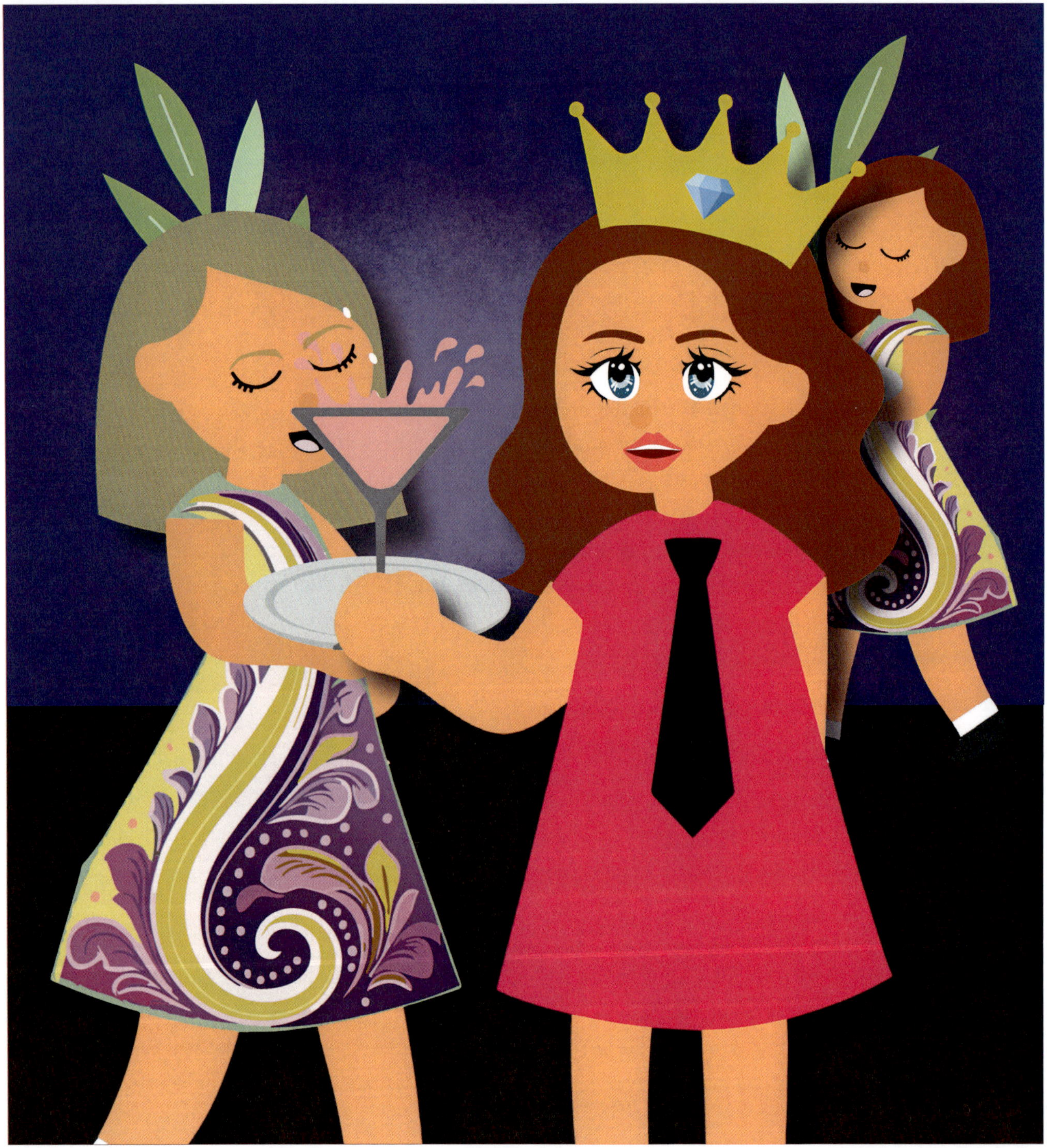

Princess Pump
AND THE AWFUL EMPLOYEES.

    Princess Pump of Beverly Hills wasn't just a princess. She was the owner of one of the kingdom's hottest restaurants. Pump took pride in her work, but lately, her pesky employees have been constantly stirring up trouble for her. A very important guest, the king of Beverly Hills, was visiting her restaurant, and Princess Pump hoped that her staff would behave for just one night.

    When the big night arrived, her best servers were nowhere to be found. That was the final straw. She was going to fire them. After searching the whole building, Princess Pump found them in the alleyway behind her restaurant. "Prince Jinx is my boyfriend!" shouted one of her waitresses. "No, Prince Jinx is my boyfriend! Shouted the other."

    "Girls, why are you missing work over a boy? And why do you keep calling him Prince Jinx? He isn't a prince," said Princess Pump. "He told us he was. That is why we are fighting over him." said the waitresses. "He most certainly is not. I run background checks on all my employees." Pump said. "Besides, you should never let a boy come between your friendship. You girls are good friends, and Jinx is just a boy." "He told us both he loved us!" The waitresses cried.

    That is when Princess Pump realized it wasn't the girls' fault and that she should give them another chance. She knew what she had to do: Fire "Prince" Jinx. The servers returned and started serving the king, who raved about his experience in Princess Pump's restaurant. Once Pump finally got rid of Jinx, her restaurant started running smoothly again.

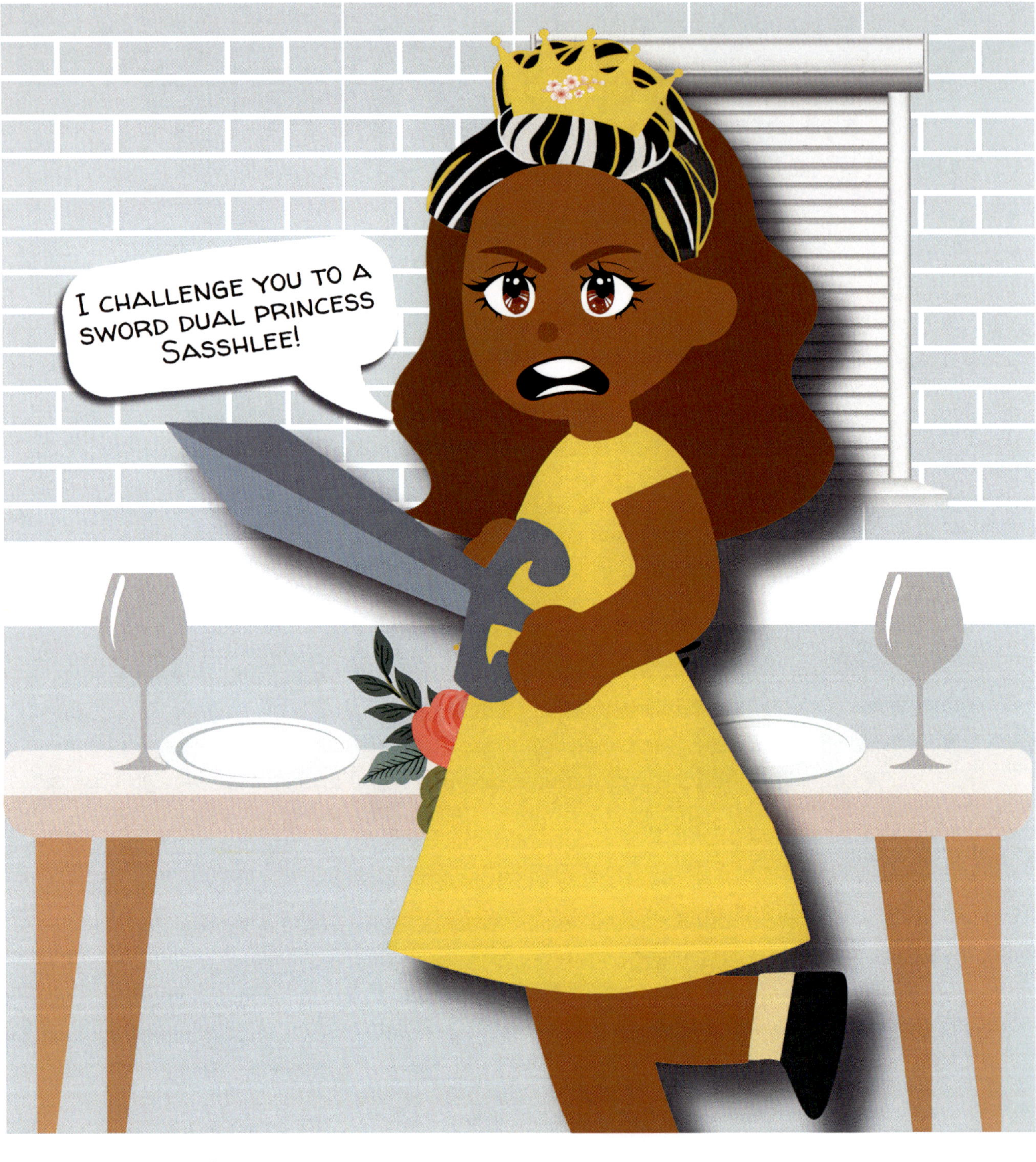
I CHALLENGE YOU TO A SWORD DUAL PRINCESS SASSHLEE!

Princess Candi
AND THE SWORD DUAL.

Once upon a time, in the kingdom of Potomac, lived a gorgeous princess named Candi. Princess Candi was newly wed to her prince, Carl. They were working hard to save gold to buy a big new castle by writing a cookbook containing the finest royal recipes of the kingdom of Potomac. Princess Candi and Prince Carl wanted to try out some of their recipes by throwing a dinner for the other princesses in the kingdom.

Although Princess Candi had been butting heads with some of the princesses, specifically Princess Sasshlee, she invited them anyway. When Princess Sasshlee arrived, she was acting very rudely. "This is my dinner party, and this is not the time to act rude!" Candi told Sasshlee. "This isn't even your castle, Princess Candi; this is your mom's castle," Princess Sasshlee snapped back.

"That is it! I have had enough! Princess Sasshlee, I challenge you to a sword dual!" The princesses began to gather to go outside for the dual when Princess Candi looked back at Prince Carl. He looked sad. "Our dinner party is ruined, and no one is going to eat our recipes," he said. That is when Candi realized she had let her anger get the best of her. She wasn't going to let a rude guest ruin her dinner party.

"You know what, Princess Sasshlee? Yes, this is my mom's castle because my prince and I are working hard for our own castle. The kingdom's economy is slow these days, and there is no shame in taking your time saving your gold! I am not going to dual you because it is a waste of time, and I need to share these recipes with the rest of the kingdom."

Princess Candi and Prince Carl's cookbook was a success, and they lived happily ever after.

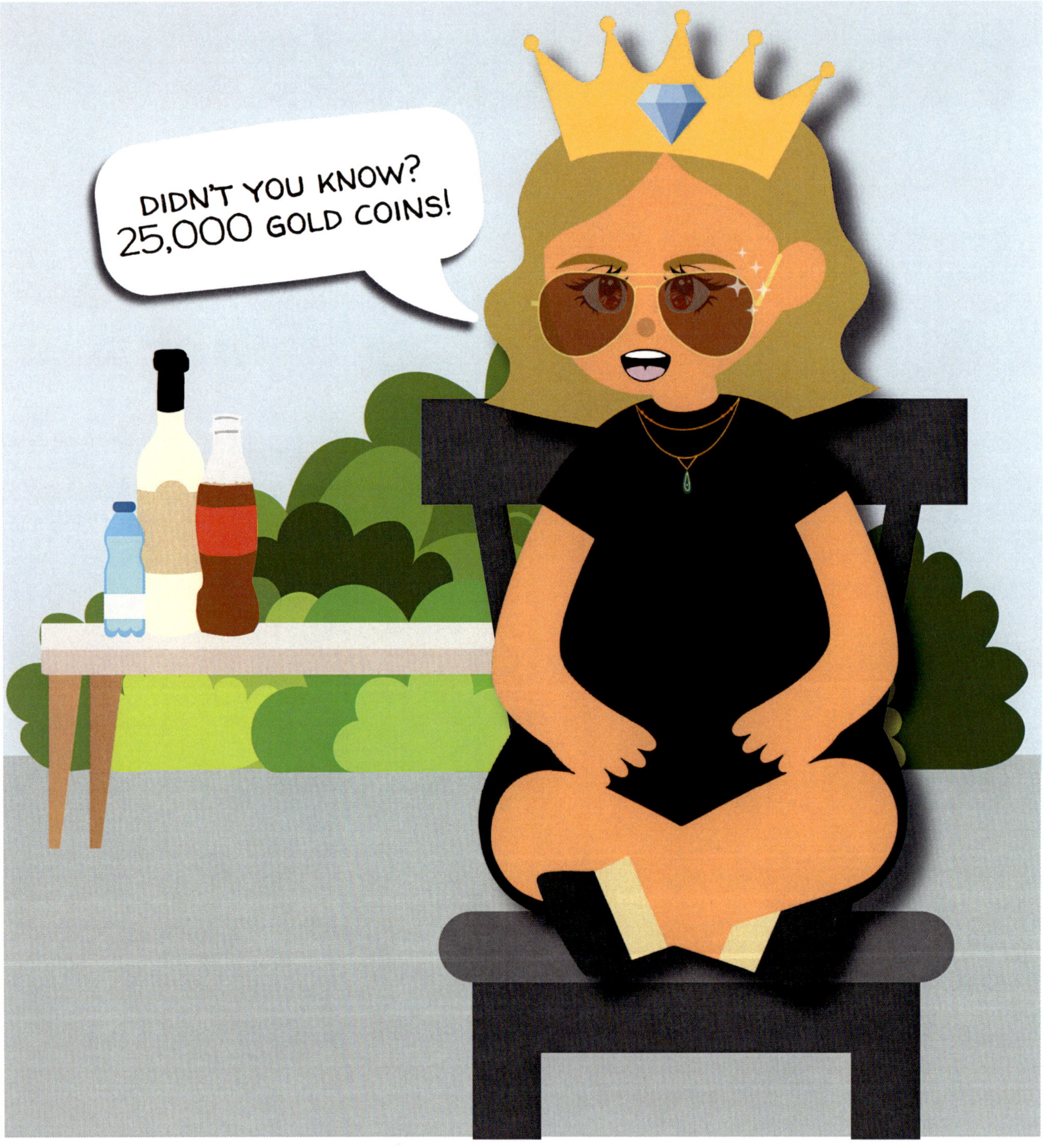
DIDN'T YOU KNOW?
25,000 GOLD COINS!

Princess Diamond
AND THE 25,000 GOLD COIN SUNGLASSES.

There was once a princess named Diamond of Beverly Hills. Princess Diamond wanted nothing more than to impress the other princesses of the kingdom. With a big royal barbecue coming up, she wanted to show up in something shiny and expensive to show off her wealth. She went to the market and asked for the most expensive thing they had. The shopkeeper handed her a beautiful pair of gold and diamond sunglasses with a price tag of twenty-five thousand gold coins.

When she arrived at the barbecue, Princess Diamond showed off her fancy sunglasses to every princess she could find. Her sunglasses were the talk of the party, just like she had planned. That was when something strange started to happen. When she looked at the royal servants working the party, she could see all their struggles, how they were only there to afford food for their families.

She lifted her sunglasses up; her magic vision was gone when they were off. She put them back on and headed home. On her way, she saw so many things she had never seen before. She saw people who had less gold than her suffering. She saw people who lived in small, run-down shacks instead of castles—things that Princess Diamond had never noticed before.

Princess Diamond felt horrible. "How could I care about impressing the other princesses when other people in this kingdom suffer?" Diamond marched right back to the market to return her glasses. She took her twenty-five thousand gold coins and gave them to people who needed them, which felt much better than wearing those sunglasses.

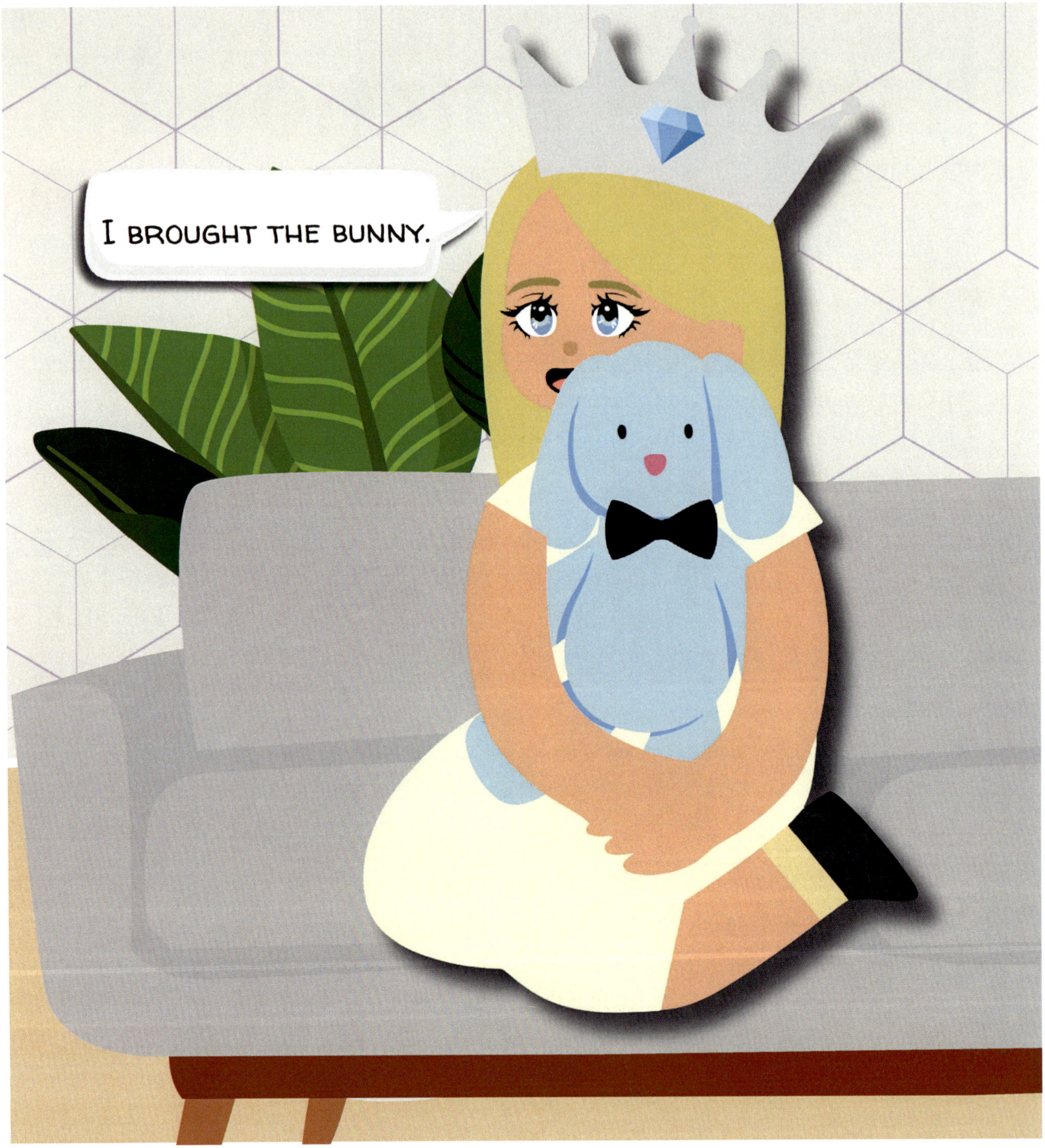
I BROUGHT THE BUNNY.

Princess Turtle
AND THE CURSED BUNNY.

Princess Turtle of Beverly Hills was no longer a princess. She was becoming a queen grandma! Other princesses around the kingdom sent gifts to welcome the new little prince. One gift, in particular, came from a princess in Queen Grandma Turtle's close circle of friends: a stuffed bunny from Princess Lips.

Something about the toy bunny felt off to the Queen, so she kept it for a little while before giving it to her new grandson. That is when Queen Turtle started noticing weird things: Glass slippers breaking, socks going missing, carriage wheels breaking. "This can't be a coincidence," Turtle thought.

Queen Turtle took the bunny to a mystical shaman, an expert in curses and bad luck. The shaman's revelation left Turtle in disbelief: the bunny was cursed. 'Princess Lips tried to curse my family?' The Queen was stunned.

The next day, Queen Turtle marched over to Princess Lips's castle and demanded why she had given her a cursed bunny. "Oh no! That must have been why it was on sale!" cried Lips. I didn't want you to judge me for buying a used bunny, so I didn't tell you there might be something wrong with it. I am so sorry, Queen Turtle."

"I would never judge you. You are my friend," said the Queen. She was mad at herself for jumping to conclusions so quickly. "Let's get rid of this bunny together," suggested Queen Grandma Turtle. Lips smiled, and off they went, better friends than before.

"I'M DONE WITH PRINCESS CHERIDITH!"

Princess Baby Gorgeous
AND THE HOT MIC FAIRY.

It was Cinco De Mayo, and all the princesses in Salt Lake City were having a great time celebrating. Princess Ren went out and threw a lavish party for all the girls. Princess Baby Gorgeous was so excited to spend time with her friends, especially her best friend, Princess Cherideth.

Everything was going great until dinner when Princess Maryloo accused Baby Gorgeous of not being a fancy princess because she liked to eat tacos! That was ridiculous; you can be a fancy princess and eat tacos. Princess Baby Gorgeous knew her best friend Cherideth would come to the rescue and defend her. Baby Gorgeous waited, and Cherideth remained silent. Princess Baby Gorgeous was so hurt she ran away to the bathroom.

"I hate Princess Cherideth! I am done with her. She is so mean!" Baby Gorgeous shouted when a magical flying microphone appeared. "Who or what are you?" the princess asked. "Why, I am a hot mic fairy," said the microphone. "Ok...and?" the princess snapped back, very annoyed. "Well, I just recorded what you said about your friend, and if you don't tell her how you feel yourself, I will tell her instead," said the fairy.

"Why would you do that?" Princess Baby Gorgeous asked. "To teach you a lesson that talking behind people's backs hurts their feelings. It is better to tell your friend how you feel." Although the princess was hurt, she talked to Cherideth anyway. Cherideth was sorry for nothing, standing up for Baby Gorgeous, and Princess Baby Gorgeous felt better for talking about her feelings. The fairy winked at Baby Gorgeous and flew away like nothing ever happened.

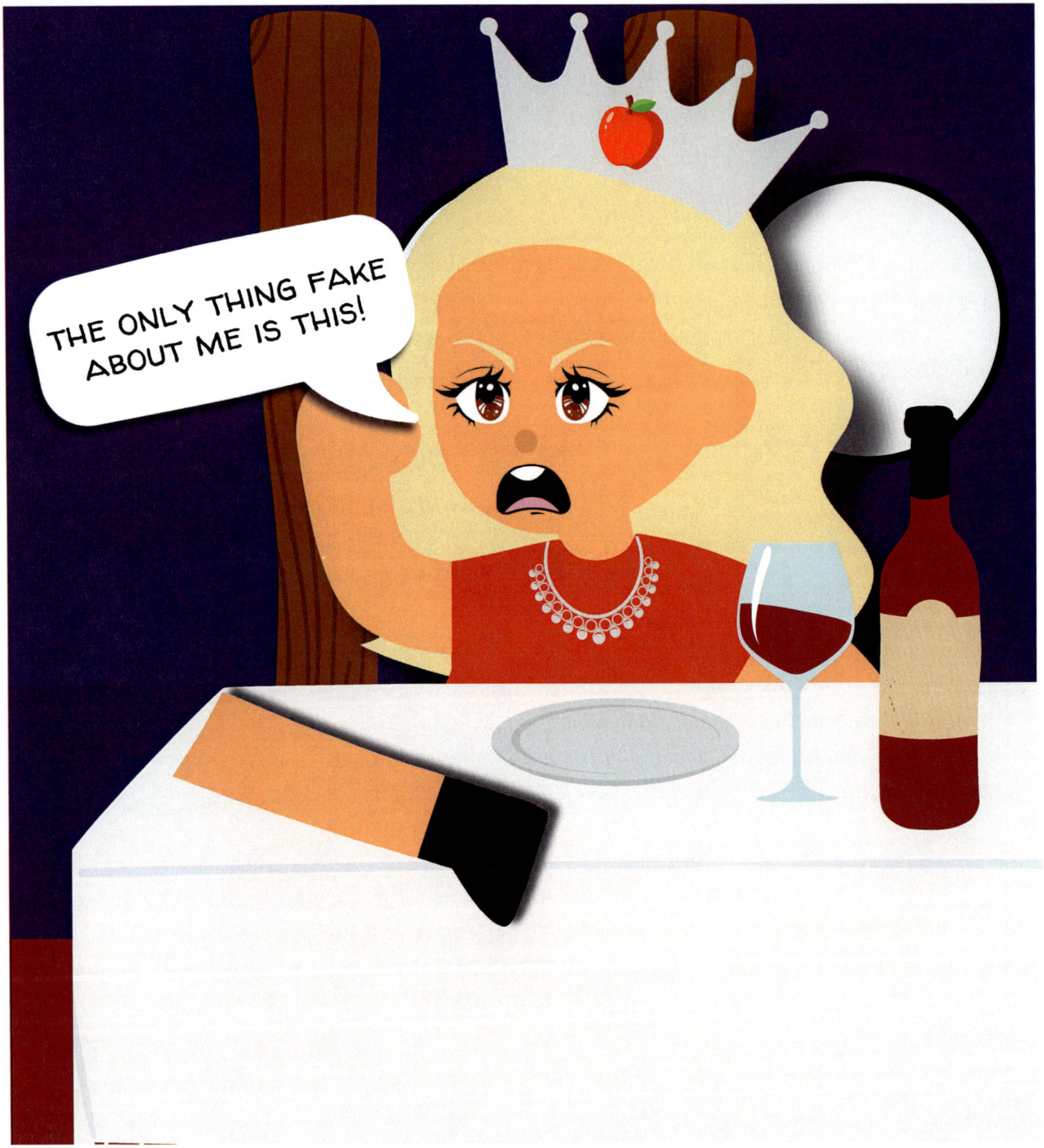
THE ONLY THING FAKE ABOUT ME IS THIS!

Princess Laviva
AND THE BIG SECRET.

Once upon a time, a princess named Laviva lived in the land of New York. Princess Laviva started hanging out with a group of close-knit princesses in New York. They all enjoyed Laviva's company but felt like something was stopping them from getting closer to her.

"Every time we try to do something fun, Princess Laviva leaves," one of the princesses complained. "She's probably off with friends she likes better," another speculated. But they were determined not to be fooled by a fake friend. "Let's confront her the next time we see her!" They agreed.

After not seeing Laviva for a few weeks, the princesses finally had their chance. "How come you mysteriously disappear every time we try to do a fun activity as a group?" said one princess. "You don't need to be a fake friend. Just say you don't enjoy doing the things we enjoy."

"A fake friend?" Princess Laviva was insulted. "The only thing fake about me is this!" She threw her wooden leg onto the table. The girls were shocked. They had misunderstood Laviva, accusing her of being a bad person when, in reality, they were the ones in the wrong for judging her. "There are many things I can't do with you princesses because of my missing leg," Laviva said. "But I like to try, and I didn't want you guys to stop inviting me out."

The girls felt awful. They should have never been so quick to jump to conclusions. "We totally understand Princess Laviva," the princesses said. "We would never leave you out, and now that we know your secret, we can be an even better friend to you." Princess Laviva was so happy she didn't have to hide her secret anymore. The group of friends lived happily ever after.

Follow the author!

Instagram: Booksbykrista

TikTok: Kristacandela

Made in United States
North Haven, CT
23 August 2024